The Trillion Dollar Business Strategy
To Make America Great Again

© 2017 by Eric Steele

ISBN-13: 978-1542448673

ISBN-10: 1542448670

The Trillion Dollar Business Strategy
To Make America Great Again

CONTENTS

1) **Objectives = pg. 5**
   a) New Avenues for the Wealthy Elites to Contribute to the Betterment of Humanity
2) **Vision = pg. 5**
   a) New Paradigm in Wealth Generation
   b) Social Responsibility
3) **Financial Strategy = pg. 6**
   a) Financial Investment
   b) Sustainability and Growth
   c) Perpetuity
4) **Products = pg. 6**
   a) Inventions
   b) Ideation
5) **Return on Investment (ROI) – pg. 19**
6) **Personal Bio = pg. 19**
   a) Inventions/Ideation/published books
   b) Skills/resume
   c) References
7) **Implementation = pg. 24**
   a) Paradigm of Abundance
   b) New Global Economic Paradigm
   c) Adopt a Community Program
   d) Adopt a Nation Program
8) **American and Global Peace and Prosperity = pg. 32**
9) **Collaboration, Investment, and Licensing = pg. 33**

Introduction

Every day in our lives, most people are struggling to survive as employees of businesses that desire to maximize profitable production. Yet the rich have figured out strategies and methods that generate great profits and executive salaries, with little obvious emphasis on social responsibility.

Fortunately, there is a sizable, albeit a relatively small group of wealthy capitalists who recognize the importance of the "rising tide" paradigm in the economics of wealth building, and how significant philanthropy (beyond public image) greatly contributes to the creation of employee consumers required for sustained corporate profitability.

This business plan offers a paradigm shift from obtaining profits at a minimal risk to the creation of a business climate and branding reputation that produces greater profits from the intelligently managed motivation of loyal workers and consumers, thereby reducing business risk through incentivizing ideation, invention and innovation.

The process of adopting motivational business practices in corporate cultures that focus on excellence and social responsibility are likely to enhance and sustain business profit growth both in the short and long term. Philanthropy and charitable giving can become an impetuous to additional wealth formation through the inclusion and contributions of highly creative individuals, whether from internal sources or from targeted niches in various viable communities.

Dedication

This book is dedicated to Donald J. Trump, 45th President of the United States of America. President Trump has clearly demonstrated that he has the vision, expertise and gumption to make America great and respected again in the world as the preeminent leader and fighter for freedom and economic prosperity… a shining light to the rest of the world.

The American dream has been created and driven by courageous entrepreneurs who believed in themselves. They have provided a world of plenty that empowered the middle-class with fulfilling careers and consumer products that provide comfort, convenience, and address their multivariate needs in a materialistic world. It's the world's visionaries, inventors, dreamers, and intelligent risk takers who have built this world from its pre-industrial latency to the technological marvels that are created daily.

It is to the spirit of the dreamers, believers, producers, and the great founders of our financial and intellectual freedoms and system that this business strategy has been written. The betterment of our global business environment is the goal of this business plan, to make our wealthy elites more capable and interested in building a better world for the future evolution of humanity.

The Trillion Dollar Business Strategy
To Make America Great Again

• 1) Objectives

1. This business plan provides **new avenues for the wealthy elites to contribute to the betterment of humanity** and contribute to the positive evolution of the human species through a comprehensive self-sustaining business plan to accomplish the following goals:
2. Create and market new inventions to generate self-sufficiency income to solve poverty.
3. Provide clean water to impoverished communities in 3rd World nations.
4. Provide goats and other sustainable livestock to the poor in 3rd World nations.
5. Build technology-based schools in poor 3rd World nations.
6. Create sustainable farming organizations to teach farming and build farms in poor 3rd World nations, modeled after Vermont farms managed by Will Allen.
7. Fund sustainable small business ventures in impoverished areas anywhere and require community ownership.
8. Cooperate with governments to stop deforestation and poaching that threaten the sustainable environment in 3rd World nations, leading to species extinction.
9. Create an interdenominational organization that solicits the cooperation of mainstream religious groups to improve acceptance, trust, ideological exchange and joint worship of God, and thereby reduces ethnic and religious tensions that cause poverty in many 3rd World nation communities around the world.
10. Help to stop religious persecution in various nations through economic incentives.

• 2) Vision

1. **New Paradigm in Wealth Generation** to create self-sustaining communities with exceptional ROI to investors.
2. Triple the value of charity trust funds within expected lifetime of investors and benefactors.
3. Create self-sustaining businesses for the poor and give them ownership, with ROI to investors.
4. Educate the poor by "teaching them how to fish" – life skills to sustain their families.
5. Invest in technologies that help the poor to become self-sustainable.
6. Fulfill the plan to tackle and reduce the causes of global poverty that include political, environmental and wildlife issues.
7. Donate to honest, worthwhile, and passionate charities that achieve good works.
8. Focus on helping the poorest children and families first.
9. Create a "rising tide" by harnessing the world's abundant resources in ecologically sound ways.
10. No more than 10% of charity trust funds for business/operating expenses, to be repaid in full.

- ## 3) Financial Strategy

1. Social Responsibility: Business Charity Plan for distribution of self-sustaining wealth in poor areas.
2. Create private charitable foundations to do good works.
3. Reinvest profits back into community businesses.
4. Invest charity trust funds in tax free government bonds with high ratings, varied maturity dates.
5. Give half of annualized maturities as direct giving to charities that help the poor.
6. Utilize the remaining half of annual maturities to invest in projects that create self-sustaining economies for the impoverished that ameliorate the causes that contribute to poverty.
7. Utilize interest rate earnings to finance administrative expenses for the charitable trust.

- **Financial Investment**

1. Demonstrate to investors, a sustainable ideation system where new concepts are discovered through synthesizing ideas and visualizing the unknown utilizing a creativity matrix.
2. Pursue multi-prong fund raising strategy, including social media, TV news publicity, crowd funding, and other investment vehicles.
3. Build linked websites to heighten awareness of program goals, for example,
   http://sites.google.com/site/creativecollaborationsgroup/
   http://sites.google.com/site/creativesynergynetwork/

- **Sustainability and Growth**

1. Successful sites are duplicated in new locations
2. Successful projects are expanded into neighboring communities
3. Market "Adopt a Community" program to wealthy investors
4. Market "Adopt a Country" program to wealthy philanthropists

- **Perpetuity**

1. The Charitable Trust shall exist in perpetuity through successful business operations and prudent national and global financial investments.

- # 4) Products

New concepts and ideas will result in a multitude of financially profitable products and services that address diverse humanitarian, environmental, ecological, consumer and market opportunities that directly contribute to improving communities and national economies.

- **Inventions** circa 1985 to 2005. In addition, 1000+ inventions/ideation from 2006-2016 available.

My forte is the ability to "think outside of the box" to create new ideas. Following are brief examples of product descriptions from over 1,500 original concepts, ideas, innovations, and inventions that I have conceived circa 1985-2005. In addition, over 1000 ideation and inventive projects from 2006 to the present are available to serious parties. Please contact me for information on confidential disclosure and licensing rights (the numbers preceding the product name denotes its position on the categorical invention lists). In a couple dozen instances, similar products are presently on the market, however, are usually inferior to my designs. Most of these concepts are at least ten years old, and only within the past decade have some similar ideas come to market. I have several additional lists of exceptional inventions with great profitmaking potential from the past decade that are ready to go upon discovery of serious investors or benefactors.

NAME OF PRODUCT: **DESCRIPTION:**

AUTOMOTIVE

1\CAR-COM	\communicate between vehicles
2\BUS-DRAGS	\sleek hi-speed bus
4\OIL FILTER CHANGER	\no slip\high torque tool
5\AUTOSHIELD DE-ICER	\automatically cleans free of ice
7\INSTA-OIL CHANGER	\no mess\1-minute oil changes
11\SAF-T-CARSEAT	\improved easy-to-use safety car seat
12\SAF-T-AIR TIRES	\never goes flat
14\SAF-T-GLASS	\non-shattering, non-splintering
18\HYDRO TURBINE ENGINE	\rotary engine that runs on water

BOOKS, SCRIPTS, SOFTWARE

1\NOTE PACK	\everything students need to keep up
3\10 Minute Quickies	\quick emotional exercises
4\Martial arts course	\new training techniques
9\Good mating	\how to video\book\self analysis
12\America Beatific	\simple cost-effective solutions
21\Continuum	\theories on moon, earth, dinosaurs, atmosphere, Bible, ice age, UFOs
29\FUNDO	\fundamentals\future\fund\fun\undo\do system of living
30\Neo-Techno	\applying techno changes to our lives
36\Invention laws	\revising archaic patent right laws
40\Population Growth	\humane ways to control world population
62\Talking to Wise men	\wisdom on life's important issues
64\Solution America	\solutions without raising taxes
65\TRUTHS	\according to God and mankind
67\Intelligent EARTH	\earth as intelligent living entity
68\Alcohol abuse	\criminality aspects of alcohol use
70\NEW MINISTRY	\synthesis of universal religious ideas
88\People of the Night	\criminal genetic predispositions

ELECTRONIC

2\DE-ICER	\window\windshield de-icer
4\SUPER-SOL	\super solar cells\5-10x more power
8\POWER-PRESSOR	\charge up your energy as exercise
16\AUTOVCR	\vcr responds to voice commands

FOOD

1\LUNCHPAK	\convenient packed lunches
3\BALANCED DIET SNACK	\essential vitamins\fiber\carbo\proteins
4\NODOPES	\fast test kit on fats\sugars\calories
7\10 MIN. COMP-SHOP MKT	\grocery shopping in 10 minutes flat

GAMES & SOFTWARE

3\Backgammon options	\changes to rules
4\WORLD DOMINATION	\based on real world scenarios
14\LAWYER TALK GAME	\telling legal lies for prizes\money
15\THE SYSTEM GAME	\how to get ahead; like super monopoly
20\REAL CARD GAME	\new card game based on probabilities
21\SURVIVING THE FITS	\obstacles to overcome to become fit
25\THE SILENT MAJORITY	\1000s of ways people fail to act
26\TERRORISM	\terrorism scenarios leave clues
27\INSANITY GAME	\making a living by being crazy
33\R RIGHTS	\illegal ways to win or trip to jail

HOUSEHOLD, CLOTHING

2\Personal assistant	\portable pin voice reminder
8\PERFECT BRUSH\ROLLER	\perfect amount of paint every time
16\INFAWARM	\survival type made to carry baby
18\ELASTICWARE GARMETS	\one size fits all\special support
19\PORTASEAT	\portable seat w ladder
20\MAXI-CAN CRUSHER	\crush dozens of cans at once
21\WATER PURIFIER	\analyze and purify as needed
27\QUAKE SHELTER	\earthquake resistant shelter
28\NOSPILL	\child-proof\no spill container

INDUSTRIAL, GOVERNMENTAL

1\Underbrush pulverizer	\chops down underbrush; prevent fires
2\Earthquake-proof homes	\construction materials & buildings
10\Wet filters	\for dryers\AC\Htrs impurities
11\Phone\computer vote	\coded true democracy

| 13\Pneumatic robots | \computer-controlled pneumatics |

LOVE, SOCIAL, PSYCHO

3\COOL-TAN SHADER	\tan through cool umbrella
5\heighten female video	\turns on women thru audio\visual
6\Uniqueness Attractant	\make cologne from lover's scent
7\Photo\love contract	\photo booths at conventions

MEDICAL\HEALTH

1\AIDSAID	\rejuvenates HIV/AIDs tainted blood
2\CPR\PROTECT	\portable CPR machine
5\NASAL-CLEAR	\insert into nostril for 5 minutes
10\PISS-ON-IT	\no splash back urinals
11\CATEPILAGE	\substitute bone cartilage
14\COMPUAID	\computer data-base of HIV/AIDS people
17\Sub-Conscious	\communication state\reprogram
19\SAF-T-CRAP	\no splash back toilets
24\Wheelchair	\collapsible\ultra-light weight
28\Breast implants	\sterilized non-infective material
29\Medi-goop	\medical adhesive for cuts\bones
33\FEMPEE	\wear under panties; works anywhere
34\Anti-Balding	\ointment reduces thinning

MONEY MAKING BUSINESSES

2\Networking Club	\for public, friendships etc.
3\Equity investment	\pooling home equities
7\Consultation network	\club to increase business
10\Minority enterprise	\networking minority business people
12\Discount consulting	\club provide low-fee consulting
13\Business salvage	\failing business leveraged buy outs
17\Manufacturer's rep	\for various products
24\Probate consultant	\administer wills for a percentage

MUSIC, MOVIES, T.V.

1\VIDEO-SING SONG	\creative sing along shows new talents
2\Laugh, Dream, Draw	\people share their vivid dreams
4\HEART-CORDS	\music that moves people to various acts
7\Al Mancini\Star Search	\ghetto\barrio star search episode
13\What's the hitch?	\game show\betting on marriage
16\New intellect show	\only the smartest: freeform ideas
20\CATS meow video	\habits of cats

RECREATIONAL, EXERCISE

1\Weight Toner	\device to lose stomach bulge
2\Friendship centers	\positive teen meeting places
6\TRAILPACK	\survivable pre-pack backpack
10\RECUMBENT BIKE	\geared\shaped for max speed & comfort
16\SKI-AID	\supports knees\legs for balance
18\HI-JUMP SHOES	\jump 10-20% higher
20\BACKBALL	\indoor batting cage\computer program
23\BIKE SEAT	\thigh\buttocks support; crotches
25\Virtual Biking	\VR programs; good for stationary bikes
26\Supermotorbike	\ultra modern & aerodynamic designs
28\Sports glove	\radio\electronic sensor w VR program
29\Electro Sparring	\boxing\martial arts cybernetic suit

SAFETY, SECURITY, SELF-DEFENSE

2\Homing device	\to track down lost kids\own code
3\Pool warning devices	\to prevent baby drowning
4\Self-defense weapon	\legal weapon slips onto hand\hidden
5\SAF-T-BATH for kids	\drown alarm worn by kids\auto unplugs
12\BABY FREE WALKER	\safe no-tip walker

SPACE & MILITARY

1\Super bullets	\high speed and accuracy bullets
2\Semi-auto pistol	\gun is 5 pieces and never jams; water-proof
3\747 Applications	\gunship\bombers\stealth\transport
6\Supersonic helicopter	\new airframe w new blade design
7\Superhummer	\transforms\multiphase engine kicks
8\Stealth Bomber\Missiles	\unique skin design w new absorbent
9\Inverted Booster Seals	\locking booster seals
10\Parachute Trans-module	\full combat armored survival units
13\Border guard	\laser & camera surveillance system
14\Blastshield	\improved concrete barriers-hybrid tech
17\Repelit	\repels RPG, mortars and grenades
20\Rightscope	\allows weapons to shoot around corners
24\AMD	\creates multiple blast zones in front of incoming missiles
29\Anti-SAM	\breakaway engine shrouds with high heat signature
30\Kill-SATS	\maneuvering killer satellites with smart bombs
34\ATV scout	\armored field ATVs, rapid airlift deployment
42\Miner	\detects buried mines from afar
45\Brainwarp	\read people's thoughts

TOYS

2\TRANS-LEGOS	\leggos that transform
3\BIG BABY	\lifelike giant-sized baby doll
4\747 Modi-Models	\plastic model planes based on 747 jet
5\No AIDS gag gifts	\condoms with clever sayings
7\BLINDSEYE	\shoot laser gun at target\sounds off

- **Ideation - sampling of more new ideas for inventions and innovations from 1995 to 2005 (some have since been invented and marketed by other innovators)**

1) spectra-light photo sensor
2) safety helmet/face shield for law enforcement
3) tennis net/let sensor
4) laser face lift with wide beam CO_2
5) gyro golf balls and golf club heads
6) water scooter
7) swim asst. mask
8) runner hydrator belt
9) baby walking pad
10) track shock starter
11) computer scoring of events
12) golf club/drive wedge
13) prayer module/increase connection to God
14) hair anchor
15) handcupps
16) facelift
17) quakeseat
18) firescape
19) smartgun
20) hairtrap
21) power snow skis
22) power water skis
23) power boards
24) Asian chess; new shapes, triangular chess board; different moves and types of power; two more pieces than chess; start from center and go out to end; other side attacks and blocks
25) gelsoles
26) micro body cameras
27) electronic/computerized water massager
28) smart TV.; features can pause while ram records, then can go to anywhere, or back to live; digital records in real-time; play delay
29) DVD/CD players that can repeat tracks per counter numbers
30) new equipment for correctional guards; body armor plus mechanical pinchers and shocker in suits
31) cat litter box; automatically cleans and sanitizes

32) security shades for car; prevents theft
33) steps that are "trip" proof
34) bug zapper that kills mosquitoes due to human heat signature
35) New line of tiger clothing; unique patterns and colors
36) redesign horseshoes; use custom hoof fitting rubber soles etc.
37) take all existing products and figure out how to improve/innovate
38) game based on life's experiences like chess/board/video game
39) pill that gets you happy, but isn't harmful and illegal

SOFTWARE:

40) computer program to beat basketball/football coaches (IBM vs. NFL)
41) computer program to assist coaching decisions or to play against actual coaches (IBM, Apple, Sun to take up challenge).
42) computer program to play actual courses against history of the great golf pros. Also, virtual reality.

VIDEOS:

43) Dikes on Bikes
44) motor home trip from city to city; live via satellite

T.V. SHOWS:

45) across America show
46) arena trials; verdict on OJ Simpson and other historic trials based upon evidence provided for popular justice
47) behind bars; life in prison, question and answer contest on inmates
48) episode for DS9; Voyager; BB5; God Speaks; they finally meet God
49) game show; if I were... bigger, taller, stronger, smarter, richer, etc., I would... prove it

MOVIES:

50) in-vitro fertilization to breed new species of more superior humans
51) Assassins; interview hired killers in syndicates, intelligence, and military and professional hit men.
52) dreams of beautiful women coming to shy guy at a table in a restaurant and kissed him passionately for no reason... comedy of lucky dork
53) humans are like animals responding to bio-chemical stimuli to our DNA physical\emotional\mental predispositions
54) space aliens are among us and they are watching us.
55) our spirits rematerialize into physical form through time travel
56) camp city; free campsites wild fun times
57) nano kill – using nanotech to target specific DNA

BOOKS:

58) photo book on cemeteries
59) photo book on motels with rating system
60) Godly thoughts: God has a message for us. Live for goodness and greatness!
   - Do your good deeds without any regards for money. Just do it.
   - Take a superior attitude of righteousness.
   - Believe in yourself
   - From God. That is the secret, as it is God's will for all.
61) Describe your ideal life, in every detail in all areas of your life and how to move from present into the future.
62) Visions of the Future; how things change to bring predictable or unforeseen outcomes
63) Militia; conspiracy scenarios that encompass Oklahoma City, World Trade Center, Heaven's Gate, OJ Simpson, and other murderers.
64) PLOTS: draw from experiences based on 100 jobs, 100 dates, and 100 residences, and the people who were met, their occupations, personalities, situations and their stories.

ESSAYS:

65) what is too old to have babies? ethical essay regarding physical condition of parents, death during early stages of child's life
   - Resulting in becoming an orphan for society to raise
   - Lifelong emotional trauma on the child.
   - Poorer quality of eggs and sperm as leading to more DNA mutations and genetic defects.
   - Dangers of childbirth on the health of the aged mother.
66) write on why workers don't get more credit for their efforts; like being
   - a homemaker who is taken for granted
   - CEOs get all the credit/profits somewhat undeservedly, despite themselves
   - proposal to UN on how nations in the world can get along better with the idea of global equal opportunity.
   - adultery is an issue of trust or deception, so should apply more to who?
   - Why are spies expected to deceive, yet to be loyal and honest?
   - What is the importance of following rules for military people?
   - Customary for soldiers to get prostitutes during shore leave and at times of war?
67) improve criminal justice system
   - penalty aspects; non-violent prisoners; restrictions
   - death penalty vs. psychological penance & rehabilitation
   - computer chip/satellite tracking of all felons on probation.
   - What is cruel and unusual punishment?
68) parody and ironies of life; ironic justice or karma
69) time is of no consequence. matter is of no consequence.
70) golfers need to use ear plugs to concentrate better/loud calls
71) cure for AIDS to be found in cow, sheep, and monkey DNA
72) earthquake computer model to Caltech, USGS, and TV stations

73) bikini basketball; co-ed bikini basketball
74) can female tennis pros compete against past male stars like Sampras?
75) new MLM concept; money goes sideways
76) what would the properties of the earth be if it were to be a cube
   - as described in the Bible, made of gold and jewels. What would the
   - gravity be; tides; atmosphere and winds, etc.
77) if it takes only half of normal intelligence to take a life, and twice the
   - normal intelligence to save a life,
   - then it would take at least thrice the normal intelligence to create a life.
78) the computer (AI) is the next superior intelligent life form
79) write questions & ideas to ideation website/APP
80) Executive Outcomes/mercenary strike force in Somalia to solve anarchy
81) nation infiltrations; CIA's role to implement U.S. foreign policy.
82) computer game fantasy; what if coach Riley coached M. Jordan?
83) magazine ad; no sex, just virtual massage only
84) what if Princess Di had married an Arab?
85) political dissident in Hong Kong, China; returns as China's ambassador
86) police use a super computer to figure out the partial license plate; match to color of car/year as in files on cars ticketed
87) Find people who can do something 1000 times non-stop:
   - counting to 1000; how long it takes; how many mistakes
   - other physical feats; sports, dance; running;
   - 1000 push-ups, pull-ups, breaking boards etc.
   - mental feats - recite 1000 facts
88) NEW MELLENIUM SOCIETY: PARADISE
   Make a society from the top people in the world; have them interbreed after their DNA analyzed. Put on island somewhere. What type of society would result? Detail qualities.

New opportunities in business every day!

1. *How to make it better of higher quality*
2. *how to make it cheaper to make, buy and use*
3. *how to make it look better, more attractive*
4. *how to make it bigger/smaller*
5. *how to make it last longer*
6. *how to make it appeal to different age groups*
7. *how to make it more powerful*
8. *how to make it stronger and more durable*
9. *how to make it more variable*
10. *how to apply to other uses*
11. *how to combine it with other products*
12. *how to redesign/re-engineer with "out of the box" ideas and concepts*

Financial Opportunities - Initial investments must concentrate on developing ideas with High Income generating MONEY POTENTIAL. Smart phone applications (APPS) are a relatively inexpensive and quick way to generate short term income. Several ideas with consumer interest that could become popular and profitable include the following:

Examples of new products:

personal appearance – rejuvenate aging, clothing keeps you warmer/colder, changes colors n patterns

e-commerce – suggested products based on buyer profiling, automatic coupons for lowest pricing

social media – voice recognition to text, voice to voice, text to voice, auto save chats, mirror of history

robotics – personal home assistant for elderly, emergency sensors for accidents/crime

finance – compound interest sharing, reinvestment protocols, social leadership financing, MLF

disease – programmable nannites, genetic bullets, stem cells, longevity epigenetics, anti-triggers

warfare – cloaking device sends opposite light wave frequencies, electro-magnetic defense shield

technology – brain interface chips, pneumatic muscle assistants, 4D printers, universal OS, real time language translators

intelligence – cloud server mining, master cloud server by mirror hacking entire web in real time

genetics – xeno-human hybrids, stem cell cures (nerve regeneration)

medical – head transplantation (full body), accelerated tissue regeneration, 3D printing of organs

animals – vocal translators in real time into human language and reverse, interspecies communications

wildlife – genetic engineering/reproduction/cloning to save endangered species

deforestation – new building materials combining rotting trees, recycled/replenished top soil

space exploration – orbiting rocket boosters/fuel stations for deep space travel to Mars and beyond

nanotechnology – blood vessel scrubbers to clean out plaque, urinates out

computers – brain chip interfaces linkage to thought controlled computing

Smart phone APPS and more

1) 24/7 cam - can edit videos/pics in real time

2) app - finding god by feeling the spirit

3) app - finding god when you most need him

4) app - have a nice day (smiley)... when people are bored or depressed or lonely

5) app - with help feature voice activated to solve all requests with links

6) app -911 smart phone button sends cops GPS coordinates automatically

7) app - facebook job alerts and swaps - make a proposal

8) app - pre-paid pizza accounts, restaurant, gasoline etc.

9) app - social connection, broadcasts profile & matches people within 500 ft.

10) app - Lie detection... ask 3 questions/stress analyze lying odds.

11) App - Love Me! = what they want, what they have, what will they give in trade, researches background to verify

12) apps that make android cellphone selfies and vids look thinner

13) big little speakers for smart phones

14) brainiacs.com = recent college students who are web savvy, creative, write apps, next big thing

15) computer program to compare players in sports and predict outcomes

16) correct pitch app... corrects singing mistakes, adds background beat and melodies you can add

17) cuddling in favorite furry costumes as a business... male or female. No sex. Guys wear jock strap.

18) decision matrix in cloud... life decisions based on personal preferences, with good vs. evil buttons

19) diet app = food label scanner... list of harmful ingredients... and calories, etc. suggests substitutes

20) encryption based on complex math formulas

21) engines that run on water or anything

22) evernote software to organize and adjust schedule automatically to priorities in real time

23) everything is a game - shall we play a game professor faulkner?

24) facebook game in real time btw fb users - with prizes and money to earn

25) ideation patents to encourage new inventions based on new ideas

26) lying game - I bet you haven't thought... who woulda thunk? Person says yes, but must describe details and audience/contestants vote to say true or not

27) god app = follow Jesus button opens decision matrix with best choice based on his teachings.

28) god app = help me god button where evil is determined and righteous path, supported by scripture

29) HAPPY PILL... builds and releases serotonin in brain

30) Hit maker = audio visual software that can blend multiple tracks of music to integrate into composition.

31) holder for cellphone cameras to make into body camera

32) instant coffee bags ... just pour in hot water - different flavors

33) Keep page open when watching TV... for new ideas based on stories & programs

34) loneliness app... auto find compatible strangers... for lunch mtg. Broadcast want to meet/chat/date/text

35) make invention ideas matrix... 8 questions

36) potential hook up app... buttons for talk, text, email, meet, share (pics, videos, links, audio etc.)

37) marathon/hiker water supply & cooling mist system = 1 pound... monitors body temp, heart rate, outside temp to determine how much hydration needed to be dispensed depending on body weight

38) mind mapping software

39) never be lonely app - anonymous phone/txt hook up... age/gender/interest driven... expertise

40) new big thing = secure operating system not apple or Microsoft

41) pet care app - all aspects of pet care categories to various types of pets, real time answers plus product links

42) photoshopper - take small pics that can be blown up but keeps pixel clarity... substitute head & body parts

43) photo recognition - Google – identifies named places, people, locations where pics taken

44) program that takes out all duplicate pages... without zapping inappropriately from other paragraphs

45) program to change date created/modified on computer files

46) software to organize files in computer, color codes folders and files, documents, etc according to categories

47) solar charging back panel for smart phones

48) telescopic zapper for cops

49) TV show = liars   use hook up to lie detector tests... host ask questions

50) voice/smart phone activated coffee/juice dispenser

51) wikiparties... read articles aloud, click on links

52) Collegebrains.com – start up connections

53) Jobswap.com – switch locations for similar jobs/skills

54) Respect.com – points traded for good deeds

55) Suggested.com – what to see, buy etc.

56) Rightorwrong.com – people ask, ethicists answer

57) Consumerwatchdog.org – give them ideas for class action lawsuits

58) Redesigning the world

INVENTIONS ON THE MARKET THAT I ALSO HAD PREVIOUSLY CONCEPTUALIZED AND INVENTED

1. Designer contact lenses
2. Gun can be trigger only by one person
3. Electrical teeth flossier
4. X-Ray glasses (fantasy in a movie)
5. Water massager
6. Vacuum hair cutter
7. Hard wall tires
8. Odorless toilet
9. Flat proof tires
10. Automatic cat litter cleaner
11. Passive stomach exerciser
12. Car wash "squeegee"
13. Gun scope to allow shooting around corners
14. Recumbent motorcycle
15. Male comfort bicycle seat
16. Full-body exerciser
17. Body balancing exercise programs
18. Child safety swimming pool alarm
19. Infant tracking & warning device
20. Wristwatch micro-computer
21. TIVO (conceptualized in 1996)

- ## 5) Return on investments (ROI) and Equity

  Targeted ROI: 1st Year ~ 10%; Yrs. 2-3~ 20%, Yrs. 4-5~ 30%, Years 6-10~ 40%
  Ownership equity: Charitable Trust = 25%, Business Operators = 25%, Investors = 50%

- ## 6) Personal Bio

  - Ideation portfolio with over 2,000 new concepts and ideas that could be developed into marketable products and services.

  - Diverse creative and management skills and experiences (please refer to resume in later section).

  - Reference letters from physicians, hospital administrators, corporate executives, university administrators, professors, teachers, counselors, friends and family are available upon request from UCLA, Olive View Medical Center, Garfield Medical Center, California State University at Los Angeles, Los Angeles County Office of Education, and other highly reputable organizations.

PUBLISHED BOOKS

I've written over 40 books and ghost-written 10 books that have been published under 5 pen names.

I believe President Donald J. Trump will prove himself to be the best President the United States of America has ever had and will eventually garner the face of U.S. currency, with a $100 gold coin to be minted after his image.

I believe President Trump has "the right stuff" to make America and the world a better place for all of humanity to insure the positive evolution of mankind by garnering in a new era of global peace and cooperation.

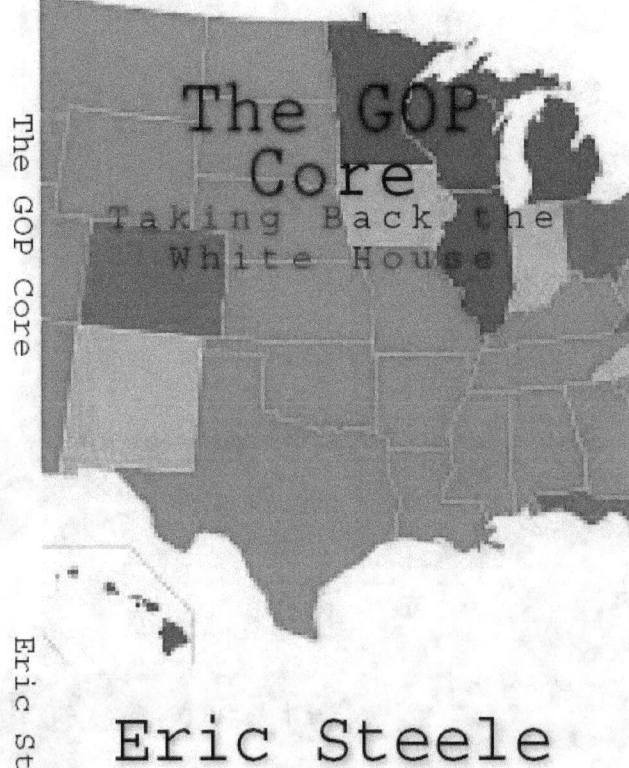

The GOP has become embroiled with in-fighting from its major philosophical factions, but are strong at the local levels, where their core values are homogeneous in rural and small town white America. The GOP mantra has been socioeconomic status quo, family values, Christian faith, anti-immigration, anti-abortion, pro-guns, anti-social programs, pro-war, pro-business wealth, and seekers of a moral society. The GOP is highly sensitive to racial issues and prefer not to give it much attention because it might alienate swing minority votes that could be essential for a White House run against Hillary Clinton or John Kerry in 2016. The GOP is attempting to walk the tight rope to avoid galvanizing minorities whose voting apathy is essential to Republican victories in state and national elections where sizeable non-white populations reside. What will it take for the GOP to win mid-term elections and to take back the White House in 2016? And what mistakes could their GOP make that would make them lose both the House majority and the White House in the next political cycle? The answers are in this book.

Barcode Area

We will add the barcode for you.

Made with Cover Creator

The GOP Core

Taking Back the White House

Eric Steele

I penned this book in 2014, and it sure appears my strategic predictions have come true with the election of a Republican President in Donald J. Trump to the helm of our great nation, the United States of America, now proud and strong again with optimism, hope, and resolve to be GREAT AGAIN!

Foreign terrorism has become the greatest threat to Western nations as a result of the regime change foreign policy of the USA. The seeds of terrorism were planted after the British Empire's collapse and resultant struggle for power by various ethnic, religious, and military groups. In addition, the decades long animosity between Arab groups and Israel has put Americans in the crosshairs of Islamic fanatics and jihadists who hate the West. Future attacks are certain, but there are steps government can take to minimize the occurrences and impact.

The Terrorists

Eric Steele

Barcode Area
We will add the barcode for you.
Made with Cover Creator

America's traditional adversarial foreign policy since WWII must keep up with the times, as technology has opened new frontiers in global competition that are being exploited by what would have been relatively weak groups in the past.

Our past policy of regime change by deposing despots has clearly left the world a less secure place. It's likely time to garner more cooperation from our allies and competitors to solve persistent conflicts that prevent the possibility of future global conflicts and war that could lead to nuclear annihilation.

I believe President Trump will lead our nation to new cultural, economic, scientific and technological heights, where America will again be the crown jewel of the world, and where products made in the U.S.A. will again command top dollar for its exceptionally good quality, durability, creativity, innovation, and superior designs.

There was once universal pride of ownership in anything "made in the U.S.A." and there's no reason why this proven paradigm cannot become the norm again under the leadership of President Trump, a proven business guru.

Who Am I? I'm a highly motivated multi-talented writer, inventor, administrator, manager and teacher who has successfully taught, trained, supervised, and managed people, multiple projects and properties over 30 years. I'm consistently able to resolve problems as they emerge by applying highly creative and innovative solutions when the "tried and true" status quo paradigms fail to adjust and compensate for unique and unexpected circumstances. I've been recognized as a results-oriented and solution-focused individual with an extensive background and knowledge in all areas of management. My areas of strength include: complex problem solving, thinking outside the box, superior research and promotion skills, flexible team player, competent in most office computer programs, excellent communications skills that include superior customer and tenant relations abilities, and resolving facilities and equipment issues.

Reference Letters

Available Upon Request from:

- Physicians, University Executives, Hospital Administrators, Professors, and Corporate Executives
- Teachers, Counselors, Friends, and Family

• 7) Implementation

- o A Paradigm of Abundance
- o A New Global Economic Paradigm
- o Adopt a Community Program
- o Adopt a Nation Program

A Paradigm of Abundance

Getting beyond the illusion of limited natural resources and recognizing the great abundance of untapped potential wealth will not be a simple task. Global coordination, vision, intelligent management, new technological applications, and sensible distribution of resources will be required to raise the global economic tide in a manner where the rich can get richer, as the poor become middle-class. Each continent and every nation possess natural wealth, some discovered and much unexplored that can be transformed to wealth in the global marketplace. Africa, South America, Australia, Canada, India, China and Russia all contain vast undiscovered and unexplored stores of valuable minerals and other natural resources that can be transformed into wealth. Even in the West, a trip through America and Europe easily shows a vast bountiful landscape of unsettled areas, farmlands, pasture, and deserts that contain undiscovered and unexplored riches beyond its present day uses. *Human progress and development need not destroy our ecosystem if we utilize eco-friendly and non-polluting processes while eliminating old and outmoded processes that contribute to global warming, species and eco destruction. The potential for new industries that create great wealth and economic growth while protecting the environment is real.*

A global eleven-point plan should be adopted by the United Nations to encourage the replacement of the conflict producing "zero-sum game" model with the realistic "abundance" paradigm. These ten points of development identify essential areas ripe for growth and wealth generation from crops, energy, minerals, recycling, and space by harnessing new technologies.

1. Global Food Production:
- Biotechnology to maximize harvests, control pests, disease and crop failures
- Scientifically improve crop rotation programs to restore land use without laying fallow
- Global computerized coordination of farm production to eliminate duplication and waste
- Global computerized coordination of distribution and pricing
- Plant new species of edible nutritious disease resistant crops that require less water
- Genetically engineer new crops that can grow even in the toughest terrains and soils
- Develop new farming techniques for harvesting the deserts, mountains, and marshlands
- Use advantageous insects to increase harvest and control pests and disease
- Use of advantageous bacteria and microbes to increase harvest and control pests
- Increase fisheries, supplemented by oceanic seeding to replenish natural populations
- Breed livestock, poultry and fish that grow faster, larger and healthier that can survive on
- a wider variety of cheaper grains, or foodstuffs not consumed by humans (e.g. weeds)
- Genetically engineer heartier livestock and the feed it requires
- Genetically engineer new breeds of livestock, poultry and fish for human consumption.

2. **Global Food Distribution:**

- Food is sold and distributed to continental warehouses coordinated by management
- cooperatives, corporations, or government agencies, according to global treaties that
- establish specific protocols and procedures
- Continental food banks distribute to member nations within its continental boundaries,
- and to private corporations in accordance to paid purchase agreements, credit/barter
- UN food charity receives five percent of all food for redistribution to impoverished areas
- Surplus food is sold to independent distributors for secondary and specialized markets
- Food prices are managed globally to derive incentive profit for distributors, predictable
- and steady income to producers, sufficient supplies and reasonable prices to consumers

3. **Oil and Gas Production, Pricing, and Distribution**

- Predictable stability of world oil prices through graduated and structured 5-10 year
- guaranteed production and pricing levels by OPEC and other oil producing nations,
- with price increases capped at no greater than five percent above world growth levels.
- Global distribution equilibrium, with wealthier nations and consumers partially paying
- higher prices to subsidize poorer nations, on a temporary basis according to a global
- growth plan designed to raise the tide for all nations.
- Excessive retail profits limitation to prevent price gouging, fraud, corruption, and
- destructive levels of inflationary greed by middlemen, where any prices exceeding
- 100% retail mark-up must be redistributed 50% to the producer, 25% to government,
- with the remaining 25% to the retailers.

4. **Mineral Exploration, Exploitation and Recycling:**

- Existing mineral uses
- precious metals production should be stabilized to meet demand
- new uses of existing supplies to enhance value of existing minerals & metals
- clean up coal, oil shale and fossil fuel production and utilization
- increased use of compressed natural gas for public transportation
- New uses from most abundant natural resources
- sand, rock and magma

- geo-thermal vents
- salt water
- kelp, weeds, prairie grass
- smog & air pollutants
- cow and animal wastes
- human waste products
- ocean floors
- lake and river sludge
- plankton
- bacteria and mold
- insects
- Recycling
- automated mega-assortment recycling centers that process by the truckloads
- organic sumps reprocessing centers
- biomass and waste

5. **Solar:**
- Energy for commercial buildings and home
- Energy to supplement vehicle hybrid engines
- Satellite focused energy beams
- More efficient solar collector arrays and solar cells
- More efficient solar collector batteries
- More efficient solar powered motors and engines
- More efficient technologies, combining various solar blade designs in hybrid large and
- mini tower arrays
- Compact designs for buildings and urban uses
- Vehicle spoilers to convert wind velocity into battery power

6. **Lightning:**
- Balloon arrays
- Discharge blimps

- Lightning rod farms
- Lightning "catch basins"

7. Hydro-electric:

- More efficient turbines at hydroelectric plants located in dams
- New technology offshore turbines to harness oceanic waves
- New technology turbines to harness strong river currents

8. Wind:

- More efficient turbines – design and technology
- Expand transmission network to tie into major electrical grids
- Identification of high wind areas that are not likely to change due to global warming

9. New Materials:

- Lighter
- Stronger
- More flexible
- More resilient
- More esthetical
- Cheaper to produce
- Found in natural abundance
- New technological applications
- New markets created by consumers
- Potential for expansive applications

10. Nuclear

- Retrofitting or closing dangerously aged facilities
- Upgrading safety with new technologies
- Freezing construction of new plants except on military bases
- Phasing out nuclear power plants as alternative energies prevail

11. Space Exploration:

- Mine the moon and Mars (but beware of potential lunar/Martian viruses/bacteria)
- Explore and harness our solar system (but beware of potential alien viruses/bacteria)

- Colonization of suitable moons and planets

A New Global Economic Paradigm

Some of these ideas may appear to be radical, but none serves to threaten the existing economic hierarchical structure. In fact, several areas are currently under development by scientists, corporations and governments. Each area of development offers the wealthy elites vast opportunities to invest in greater profits, as the world's population benefits from the new technologies, materials, and global economic stability that will be spawned. The pursuit of abundance is natural and expansive. The fixation on the illusory zero-sum game model serves only to limit the production of wealth, as it casts billions into lives of poverty. Making the right choice for either progress or continued conflict will determine either the survival or extinction of humans, while generating a vast surplus of wealth for the global elites or fomenting destruction.

The pursuit of abundance will harness the great resources and technologies spent on military defense, and permit those investing in the next war instead to find greater purpose and power by investing in tomorrow's peaceful technologies based upon similar technologies now utilized for weapons design and production. Investing in abundance is "win-win" for everyone; the rich, poor, middle-class, the military, defense industries, high tech corporations, low tech companies, manufacturing sector, service sector, and governments of every nation on Earth. Nay-Sayers will always offer reasons why investing in abundance is impossible, but they'll be left behind, clinging on to old outmoded models as if the Earth is the center of the universe. Along with this new millennium, we must look to the future, as the methods of the past are behind us, and dragging them along only slows progress and burdens humanity.

What a wonderful world that we could have because the *human potential* is for greatness, as our wonderful minds and bodies possess. As a species of intelligent beings, we know what we must do to ensure our survival on this small planet. We possess the technology to improve the living conditions of every person on earth, while cleaning up and protecting our natural environment. We possess the natural resources, if appropriately distributed to ensure that every human being will have adequate shelter, food, and medical care throughout their lifetimes. We possess the ability to create meaningful employment that permits individuals to develop self-respect and sustainable lives. What holds us back is the same genetic traits that first helped early humans to survive... fear, clannishness, prejudice, greed, power lust and violence.

As a species, our primal genetic code has not evolved much over the past 200,000 years, since new races evolved from Africa. The primary changes have been superficial and insignificant, primarily the color of hair, skin, and eyes; which have become the greatest source of division and conflict due to wars based upon ethnic and racial conflict. On the inside, humans are almost indistinguishable from each other. No human has wings or gills that function. Our skeletal, muscle, pulmonary, excretory and circulatory systems are structured the same, and function exactly in the same way for everybody. When we, as an enlightened species finally come to grip with the destructive nature of greed and warfare primarily to service power and greed, then humans may stand a good chance to embrace a bright future among the planets of the universe, as we are designed to do.

An economic paradigm shift is possible, where global economic prosperity is a goal within reach, as the rich become richer and the poor become middle-class. History clearly shows that societies with healthy middle classes are economically, socially and politically stable as middle-class people are maintainers of society. The economic wisdom of the past and present states life is a "zero-sum game." This economic model suggests that there is a limit to resources, and conflict arises as a direct result of distribution hierarchies and that create great disparities among the world's populations. The wealthy global elites own and exploit world resources, as poverty envelops most of the world's population. It's a matter of history that the zero-sum economic model has created much turmoil, as successive civilizations conquered, plundered, and destroyed other cultures, only later to meet their own demise. As greed and the zero-sum game model interact, artificial shortages are created by those who hoard, to the detriment of those in greatest need. The zero-sum game of "greed versus need" has resulted in a world where the downtrodden and powerless are willing to fling their lives into destruction, with the hopes of destroying perceived symbols of the ruling class of wealthy elites. History also has clearly shown that the poor revolt against the rich when they have nothing else left to lose. Warfare has almost always resulted from a combination of greed or destitute and wanton greed has been the motivating force that has had a highly disproportionate effect on destroying our little planet.

A new economic paradigm that recognizes abundance must envelop the world order to eliminate the seemingly perpetual zero-sum game paradigm. We need not look too far to discover that life, our earth, and our universe is filled with limitless abundance! Certainly, there exist sufficient natural resources to support a reasonable human population of less than ten billion people, if resources are properly exploited and distributed. Management and distribution of world resources should eliminate waste, conserve the ecosystem, and intelligently use natural resources through technological enhancements to solve even the most persistent and perplexing human problems. The rich, who can provide capital and skills to optimize world resources, can become richer, as poverty is eliminated, and a growing global middle-class becomes the consumers of production that is owned by the wealthy elites. It's a win-win paradigm that can be utilized to improve our environment and to save for world for our future generations of all sentient life on planet Earth.

It is essential to examine the basic premise that created and perpetuates the zero-sum game mindset. During humans' earliest times, each day was a struggle for survival, as food, water and other usable natural resources appeared to be limited and in short supply, often requiring hoarding and defending. As civilizations and nations evolved from tribes and city-states, the fear of shortages continued, as human conflict, violence, and warfare sought to distribute the seemingly limited human resources to the powerful, creating a class of wealthy individuals. In today's world, nations struggle to protect their "national interests" as globalization of economic structures by multi-national corporations and the wealthy elites threaten to subjugate the economic interests and survivability of poorer nations. The zero-sum game continues to place large armies face to face across imaginary boundaries, waiting for the order to attack, destroy, kill, and plunder. Conflicts persist around the world; Korea, Iraq, Israel, Palestine, Liberia, Somalia, and Libya, just to name a few, with dozens more "hot spots" festering and waiting to be ignited by competition for the illusory limited wealth in the zero-sum game.

Adopt a Community Program

America's inner cities are in dismal decay with widespread blight and crime. Government sponsored entitlement programs have done little to solve the longstanding problems of homelessness, poverty, and violence that plague almost all major cities in the United States. Wealthy individuals and private venture capitalists stand to make huge profits were they to implement innovative economic self-sufficiency programs that serve to engage community members with proportionate ownership of local businesses that serve their communities.

Adopt a Nation Program

There are numerous underdeveloped and developing nations around the world who need investment of capital to improve their economies. There are 70 nations whose GDP (2014) was below $14 Billion USD. The world's elite billionaires individually or in collaboration have sufficient wealth to literally buy the land from these national governments in exchange for building their economies. This is one avenue to eliminate poverty and other environmental and inhumane situations that abound in poor nations without proper infrastructure and sufficient exploitation of their economic resources.

• 8) American and Global Peace and Prosperity

The election of President Donald Trump is a godsend in many ways. He brings unabashed confidence and an independence from political correctness that has been refreshing to most Americans who supported him. Americans must unite behind President Trump to give him the support and mandate to make American great again! America was the burning torch for freedom and economic prosperity after beating two enemies on two fronts oceans apart during World War II. Now these past enemies, Germany and Japan, have become staunch American allies. Russia and China on the other hand were America's allies during the Great War, but the adoption of the communist political system eroded the war time alliances and dampened cooperation between the West and the communists.

We are now at an opportune moment in the history of mankind... the possibility that our expert negotiator President Trump will be able to bring about a lasting world peace with prosperity for all. No other President has had the keen understanding of finances, investments, and the pulse of the people who elected him as President Trump has clearly demonstrated. He has the wits and ability to do many great things, and we should support his effort to implement policies that are good for America, but also good for the world. God bless President Donald Trump, and Godspeed!

• 9) Collaborations, Investment, and Licensing Agreements

Please contact me by email (**ericsteeleideation@outlook.com**) should you desire to further explore invention details; new ideation contained in this business plan and additional concepts or would like to invest or participate in building wealth while empowering downtrodden communities to become self-sufficient and profitable. Let's make lots of money rebuilding our world in a paradigm of abundance, hope, and profitability.

In general, my pricing structure is 1-2% for ideation, and 2.5-4.5% for developing concepts into patents. Compare this low "commission fee" structure to the 6% charged by real estate agents, 10% as church tidings, 15% by professional managers, 25% charged by credit card companies and the IRS for late fees, and 30-50% charged by attorneys, little of which serve to generate perpetual income to investors and customers.

All fees are subject to future negotiation; consequently, for 1-4.5% of eventual gross profits (no upfront or front loading of fees), and investors gain the lion's share of gross profits. You may also review new business and collaborative concepts at the following sites:

https://sites.google.com/site/creativecollaborationsgroup/

https://sites.google.com/site/creativesynergynetwork/

www.ingramcontent.com/pod-product-compliance
Lightning Source LLC
Chambersburg PA
CBHW081315180526
45170CB00007B/2718